INTO THE JUNGLE

WRITTEN BY JONI PREW
ILLUSTRATED BY LISA M LAKE

HAPPY DISCOVERY!
Enjoy ♡
Joni Prew
Lisa M Lake

INTO THE JUNGLE

Dedicated to teachers everywhere

All rights reserved.
No part of this book may be reproduced, stored in a retrieval system, or transmitted in any form, by any means, including mechanical, electronic, photocopying, recording, or otherwise, without the prior written consent of the author or publisher.

Published by IngramSpark
Words ©2021 Joni Prew
Illustrations ©2021 Lisa M Lake

ISBN: 978-0-578-92244-7
BISAC: JNF003300
First printing

Into the Jungle

written by Joni Prew
illustrations by Lisa M Lake

copyright 2021
circletimeproductions.com

Into the jungle

flying **up** into the trees

I spy a toucan

as colorful as can be

Into the Jungle

slithering on the ground

I spy a snake

He is big and brown

Into the jungle

resting **under** the brush

I spy a leopard

who is in no rush

Into the jungle

hopping over the plants

I spy a dart frog

slurping up ants

Into the jungle

sleeping **in** the shady tree

I spy a sloth

off in a dream

Into the jungle

swinging **out** on a limb

I spy a monkey

and I smile at him

Into the jungle

trumpeting **by** the water hole

I spy an elephant

bathing was his goal

Into the jungle

All around

You will find...

Big animals,

Small animals,

So many kinds....

The End

Book description

Learning is so much fun when put to rhythm and rhyme. Into the Jungle is an amazing habitat book for young children. Into the Jungle teaches early learners inferencing, directional words and rhyme while discovering animals of the jungle.

Fabric art illustrations add texture relief to the jungle habitat that animals live and adds dimension to camouflaged animals' environments. It is sure to inspire follow up art projects.

Teacher/Parent Ideas

* Before reading begins, BRAINSTORM animals the children already know live in the jungle.

* On each page of text, read the first two lines and allow children to use clues and directional words (in color) to INFER any animals that could complete the stanza.

* On the last page, what animals can you find? Have the children use directional words such as in, on, under, by, over to describe the location of each animal. There are 8 kinds of animals... (monkey, 2 cranes, 2 birds, hippo, lion, mouse, beetle, and a giraffe).

Book extension ideas

* Create a class or individual book of jungle animals... Here's an example of a very simple one:

Into the jungle

I spy _____

* Create a jungle collage by layering different patterned papers and applying an appropriately positioned picture of a jungle animal.

For more **Into the Jungle** activities:
www.circletimeproductions.com/intothejungle

CPSIA information can be obtained
at www.ICGtesting.com
Printed in the USA
BVHW022159110621
609378BV00001B/1